SIMPLY
STRENGTH

HB

HINKLER
BOOKS

Creative Director: Sam Grimmer

Editor: Hinkler Books

Design: Katherine Power

Photography: Ned Meldrum

First published in 2004
by Hinkler Books Pty Ltd
17-23 Redwood Drive
Dingley Victoria 3172 Australia
www.hinklerbooks.com

© Hinkler Books Pty Ltd 2004

Printed and bound in China

ISBN 1 7412 1510 2

CONTENTS

INTRODUCTION

How many times have you said to yourself, 'I really need to start an exercise program', but never followed through with it? How many times have you started an exercise program and stopped within weeks? Why?

Is the reason for this behaviour due to a belief that getting any benefit from an exercise program requires much time, effort and money? More than you are able or willing to spend?

If I were to say to you that you could get fantastic results with your health, strength, fitness and body shape without spending a fortune, devoting seemingly endless hours or buying expensive and complicated equipment, would you believe me? I hope so, or you have wasted your money buying this book!

It is true that if you want to get great long-term results out of your training then a consistent effort is required. However, for most people, two to three hours per week is all the time that needs to be devoted. A pair of appropriate shoes, some comfortable clothes and an open mind are the keys to your new body and the start of your new life.

The four major elements involved with long-term physical change are:

- Psychology – changing your thinking, attitudes and self-belief
- Training – for strength and cardiovascular fitness
- Nutrition – eating for enjoyment, energy and success
- Lifestyle – addressing limiting factors and making time for the important things.

Obviously the main focus of this book will be strength training, but I will also outline suggestions for the other vital components.

Simply Strength outlines strategies for you to gain fantastic results in the comfort of your own home. All that is required is a small time commitment, minimal equipment, some know-how, an open mind and the desire to change for the better.

THE BENEFITS

For many people, the main benefits of taking on an exercise regime, such as that outlined in this book, are:

- reduction in body fat
- increase in lean muscle tissue and body tone
- increase in strength, endurance and cardiovascular fitness
- increase in energy levels
- improvement in the condition of skin and hair
- postural improvements
- flexibility improvements
- improved sporting performance and self confidence.

Many physical benefits of exercise are not obvious to the observer. But they are crucial for living a healthy, functional and happy life. They include:

- increase in core and joint stability and therefore a reduction in pain and injuries caused by a lack of this stability
- reduced risk of heart disease, diabetes and other serious medical conditions
- increased metabolism, which in turn will increase the rate at which your body burns fat
- improved sleep patterns
- increased ability to recover from injury and illness
- improvement in brain chemistry.

A variety of positive associated effects of exercise can include:

- reduction in stress
- increased productivity in every area of your life
- increased social participation
- more consistent moods
- more fulfilling relationships, due to having more energy
- greater enjoyment of and achievement in life
- increased self image, self esteem and self confidence.

Even if you only experience a small percentage of the above, won't your world become a better place?

If the answer is 'yes' then read on.

TRAINING CONSIDERATIONS

When you start an exercise program, I'm sure your intentions aren't to go for a short time and then stop. Yet, for most people, this is exactly the case. In fact, of all the people who join a gym, only 10 per cent will still be exercising regularly 12 months later. Of the people that discontinue exercising, the vast majority give up within the first three months!

Think about the reasons why you may have stopped an exercise program in the past. Do they include: boredom; perceived lack of results; soreness or injury; lack of time, money or proper equipment; personal issues or an important event in your life (such as a wedding or moving house); personality clashes with your trainer; or simply poor weather?

I'm sure there are many more reasons that you can think of. The question is, and you have to be truly honest with yourself here, are these legitimate and justifiable reasons for you to stop exercising?

If the answer to that question is 'yes', then this book will help guide you in dealing with the particular issue or issues. If the answer is 'no', then the best advice I can give is that you, and no-one but you, is responsible for the outcome you attain. The sooner you take responsibility for your actions, the sooner you will start on the track to long-term success.

Okay, now I've got that off my chest, let's look at the things you must consider before you begin. The aim is to develop new lifestyle habits that will last a lifetime and continue to create balance, happiness and fantastic results until your time on this earth is done.

PREPARING TO START

The very first question you must ask yourself before starting any regime is: 'Can I maintain this long term?'. To ensure this is the case, make sure you can answer 'yes' to the following questions:

Do I really want to start an exercise regime?

This must be a decision made for the right reasons – because you really want to change not because someone says you should.

Am I prepared to commit to this long term?

You need to understand that you are about to go through this change for a lifetime, not just until summer! You need to understand that there are no quick fixes and be willing to take as much time as necessary to change your thinking and gain the body and life you desire.

Do I enjoy the exercise I am doing and is there enough variety?

If you don't enjoy it, no matter how hard you try, it won't last. Not only will variety increase your enjoyment and motivation, but your body will benefit from a range of exercise styles and techniques.

Have I made my exercise regime a priority in my life?

To be successful with your training it has to be done consistently.

This means the times you allocate for exercise must have a high priority and other commitments must be arranged around them.

Am I doing appropriate exercise for my goals?

If you are trying to lose body fat, then as good as it might be, doing yoga three times a week is not the most effective way to achieve this goal. Make sure you understand what the most effective and enjoyable exercise for your needs is.

Am I progressively increasing the intensity and/or workload of my exercise?

If your goal is to continually improve, then as you adapt to your exercise, you need to gradually and progressively increase the load.

Am I giving myself adequate recovery?

Recovery and rest are just as important for your body as the exercise. This is where your body and mind recuperate, regenerate and rebuild.

Am I eating appropriately?

This is a hard question to answer and one that I will touch on in the 'Nutrition Overview' section of the book. However, it is crucial to understand that regardless of how well you are training, if your eating doesn't complement your lifestyle then you will sacrifice the results you can potentially achieve.

WORKOUT CONSIDERATIONS

There are several considerations to ensure that your strength training workout is as effective as it can be.

TECHNIQUE

For maximum benefit and reduced risk of injury, make technique a priority. The method for each exercise will be described in further detail later. Spend the first week or two of the *Simply Strength* program at an easier level and ensure that your technique, posture and body awareness are second nature.

SETS AND REPETITIONS

Each single repeat of a movement is called a repetition and each group of repetitions is a set. Each exercise will have a target for repetitions and sets to be completed in each workout.

LOAD

The resistance applied to each repetition is referred to as the load. Increasing the weight that is lifted, slowing down a movement or changing body positions can increase the load and therefore the intensity of the movement.

SPEED AND CONTROL OF MOVEMENT

All strength movements must be performed at a slow and controlled speed for maximum effect, particularly the lowering phase where the tendency is to let gravity take over. Each repetition should take between two and four seconds.

PROGRESSIVE OVERLOAD

To increase strength, a gradual and progressive increase in workload is required. Once you have achieved the required repetition range for each set, the load needs to be increased. After a load increase, the goal is to gradually increase repetitions to the set target and then increase the load again. Each exercise has a series of progressions so you are aware how to increase the load. Your set and repetition requirement will be anywhere from two to four sets, depending on your fitness and strength levels.

WARM-UP

To ensure the appropriate muscle groups are warm and prepared for an increased load, one or two easy warm-up sets will be performed for each exercise.

TRAINING INTENSITY

Once the warm-up is complete, the working sets follow. To ensure your body is getting the best possible workout, and hence gaining the most benefit, it is imperative that during these working sets you take your muscles to a point they haven't previously been. This may mean working to muscle failure.

TRAINING DIARY

Keeping an accurate record of all loads, repetitions and sets will ensure that progressive overload can be consistently achieved.

BREATHING

Many people hold their breath when strength training, which is not good for blood pressure.

Remember to breathe as normally as possible, and, if possible, breathe out on the exertion part of the movement and breath in on the return movement.

TRAINING FREQUENCY

Depending on your training history, the program can be done from one to three times per week.

If frequency is two or three times per week, make sure you have at least one full day off in between sessions.

REST BETWEEN SETS

As a general rule, allow one to two minutes recovery between sets of the same exercise, or exercises involving the same muscle groups.

SUPER SETS

To save time in a strength workout, it is possible to choose a pair of exercises (involving different muscle groups) and alternate sets between them until they are complete. As different muscles are being used for each exercise, minimal rest between sets is required.

Many of the considerations I have introduced here will be clarified later in the book. To get the most out of this program, you need to understand each of the above points.

CORE STABLISATION

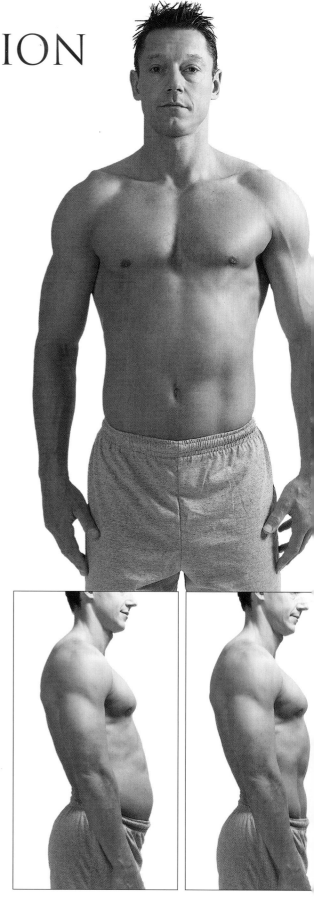

Before getting into the Simply Strength program I want to touch briefly on this important area.

By far, the most common injury experienced by people whether exercising or not is lower back pain, soreness or tightness. Consequently, other referred conditions may become apparent and affect the daily function of a person.

I am not going to cure your back pain, but I do want to give you a couple of simple hints that may help prevent or manage lower back discomfort.

Many people shy away from certain exercises because they believe they aggravate the lower back. In fact, it is usually only exercises done incorrectly or without proper stabilisation that will create further problems.

When talking about stabilisation we are referring to the foundation of strength. Let me give you an analogy. What would happen to a house, no matter how well it was constructed, if it were built on a swamp? Obviously it would sink. Any house needs proper foundations if it is to stand up. The human body is the same. Trying to build muscle on a weak foundation without adequate stabilisation will inevitably lead to injury.

TRANSVERSUS ABDOMINIS

The main muscle responsible for core (lower back) stabilisation is called the transversus abdominis (TVA) muscle. This muscle is the deepest of the three layers of abdominal muscles and lies beneath the external and internal obliques. It is the key to abdominal contraction and can be thought of as your own natural muscle corset.

Studies confirm that the transversus abdominis is prone to dysfunction in people with lower back pain. If we can strengthen this muscle, then we go a long way to preventing a lifetime of lower back pain, associated injuries and ongoing frustration.

The activation of the transversus abdominis is a delicate but relatively simple exercise. The strengthening of this muscle, as with any other, takes a consistent effort over a period of time.

1 Take in a deep diaphragmatic breath (i.e. fill the abdomen, not the chest).

2 Hold your breath momentarily and draw your belly button towards your spine. (It is important, during this movement, that you do not change the shape or position of your spine.)

3 Once your belly button is held in this new position, commence breathing normally.

4 Adopt and attempt to maintain this position at all times. (Especially when performing strength exercises, lifting movements or any other actions where your lower back is prone to aggravation.)

THE GLUTEALS

This group of muscles (located in your buttocks) play an important role in lower back support and stability. The gluteals, when activated, produce movements very similar to the muscles of the lower back.

This means that if we can learn to activate our gluteals at appropriate times (for example when lifting or when pushing above the head), we can take an enormous amount of stress off our lower back.

Activating this group of muscles is easy. Imagine you have a $100 note between your buttock cheeks and you don't want anyone to get it!

This is the simplest description I can give. The aim is to squeeze the gluteals together, make them as hard as you can, so you may then safely lift from the ground, push above your head, do a push-up or any other activity where the back is arched.

Tight hip flexor muscles may inhibit gluteal activation. These are opposing muscles and are quite inflexible in many people. It may be necessary to spend some time stretching these muscles in order to get the most out of your gluteals. I have outlined an effective hip flexor stretch in the 'Stretching' section of the book.

THE PROGRAM

The following group of exercises make up an effective full body workout that can be completed in the comfort and privacy of your home.

The assumption is that you have no gym equipment such as dumbbells, bars, benches, exercise balls or other aids. If you do, feel free to incorporate them as, although not essential, they will increase the effectiveness of the session.

All you really need is:

- some floor space
- comfortable clothes
- training shoes
- a large towel
- drinking water
- music that you enjoy
- household props and items as described in each exercise.

Each of the exercises in the *Simply Strength* program will have a description of:

- the muscles responsible for the movement
- exercise techniques – please ensure you read this book carefully, watch the DVD, understand and practise.

Remember that your technique and posture are the priority rather than the amount of weight lifted.

- equipment or props needed (if any)
- a target for sets and repetitions – remember your aim is to achieve the repetition target for each set and then increase the load
- exercise progressions – so that you can gradually increase the load. Select an easy option for the warm-up sets

COMMON PROGRESSIONS

These are ways to increase intensity for all body movements and can be used in conjunction with the specific progressions described for each exercise. They will not be described with each exercise, but can be applied with all of them. These include:

- slow reps – the slower your movements, the greater the force needed to sustain the movement (these can take between four and 10 seconds per rep)
- pause reps – by stopping and holding a repetition at a certain stage of the movement, again the intensity is increased (these can last anywhere between one and 10 seconds, depending on your level)
- partial reps – restricting the range of movement of repetitions will increase the degree of difficulty
- combination – any combination of the slow, pause and partial reps will further increase the load under which you can place your muscles.

Okay team, here we go!

PUSH UPS

Muscles involved: *pectorals (chest), anterior deltoids (front of shoulders) and triceps (back of the upper arm).*

TECHNIQUE

1 Adopt a prone position (face down) with your hands on the floor, fingers forward and arms and body straight.

2 Your hands should be directly below your shoulders and slightly wider than shoulder width.

3 Ensure your TVA and gluteals are activated. Your head should be in strict alignment with your body. Maintain a straight body position.

4 Slowly lower chest to the floor to a point where your elbows are at right angles.

5 From this lowest point, push the heel of your hands into the floor and slowly return to the starting position.

6 Repeat the movement.

TARGET FOR SETS & REPS

- 1st set — 15 easy reps
- 2nd set — 12 moderate reps
- 3rd set (optional) — 10 hard reps (work to failure)
- 4th set (optional) — 8 to10 hard reps (work to failure)

1 Put your hands against a wall with your body almost upright.

2 Put your hands against the dining table or the back of a chair with your body on a 45 degree angle.

3 Put your hands on the floor, rest on your knees.

4 Put your hands on the floor, rest on the toes with your body straight.

5 Put your hands on floor, feet raised on a chair, your body straight.

Bent Over One Arm Row

Muscles involved: *Latissimus dorsi, rhomboids and trapezius (upper back), rear deltoids (back of shoulder), biceps (front of upper arm)*

Technique

1 Stand next to a coffee table or chair.

2 Place your left knee on the coffee table or chair and your left hand on the same coffee table or on another chair. Keep your right foot on the floor.

3 Right leg should be straight and the right foot about 30 to 50cm from the table or chair.

4 Ensure that your shoulders are back, hips are square and that your back is flat.

5 Activate your TVA.

6 Grasp the weight in your right hand and hold it, with your right arm straight, just off the floor.

7 Keeping your shoulders level, lift the weight vertically, raising your right elbow to the ceiling and bringing the weight to your hip bone.

8 Squeeze your right shoulder blade towards your spine.

9 Slowly lower the weight back to the starting position and repeat.

10 Once a complete set is performed with your right hand, repeat on the other side.

Target for Sets & Reps

- 1st set — 15 easy reps each arm
- 2nd set — 12 moderate reps each arm
- 3rd set (optional) — 10 hard reps each arm (work to failure)
- 4th set (optional) — 8 to 10 hard reps each arm (work to failure)

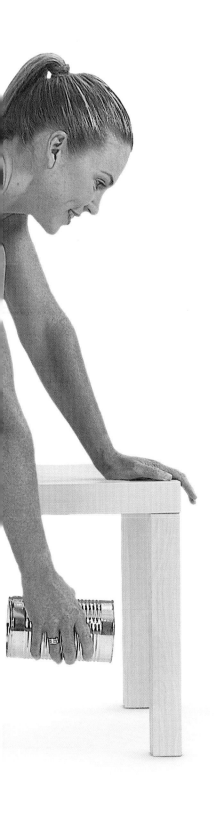

PROGRESSIONS

1 Start with a light weight – a can of food, small water bottle etc.

2 Increase weight – use a larger water bottle, brick etc.

3 Further increase weight – use a sports bag with handles and fill with whatever will give an appropriate weight.

4 Keep using the sports bag and fill it with more or heavier contents.

SHOULDER PRESS

Muscles involved: *middle deltoids (shoulder), trapezius (upper back), triceps.*

TECHNIQUE

1 This exercise can be done either seated or standing. If seated, use a back support and ensure that your back is fully against it. If standing, keep your legs slightly bent and ensure that your TVA and gluteals are activated.

2 Start the exercise with your elbows bent and to your side.

3 Take an equal weight in each hand and lift to shoulder height, with palms facing forward.

4 From this position, press the weights vertically until your arms are extended above your head.

5 Return to the starting position in a slow and controlled manner.

6 Repeat the movement.

TARGET FOR SETS & REPS

- 1st set   15 easy reps
- 2nd set   12 moderate reps
- 3rd set (optional)   10 hard reps (work to failure)
- 4th set (optional)   8 to 10 hard reps (work to failure)

PROGRESSIONS

1 Start with a light weight – a can of food, small water bottle etc.

2 Increase weight – use a larger water bottle, brick etc.

3 Further increase weight – use a sports bag with handles and fill with whatever will give an appropriate weight.

4 Keep using the sports bag and fill it with more or heavier contents.

SIDE LYING ROTATOR CUFF

Muscles involved: *this is a fantastic exercise for the small muscles that stabilise and hold the shoulder joint in place. They are called infraspinatus, teres minor and supraspinatus.*

TECHNIQUE

1 Lie on your right side on the floor with your left leg forward for stability and your head resting comfortably in your right hand.

2 Grasp a light weight in your left hand.

3 Place your left elbow on your left hip bone and bend this arm to 90 degrees.

4 Pushing down with your left elbow into your hip, rotate your shoulder and lift the weight as high as possible.

5 At all times keep your left elbow joint in contact with your hip and its angle at 90 degrees.

6 Slowly return the weight to the starting position.

7 Repeat the movement.

8 At the completion of the set with your left arm, repeat with your right.

TARGET FOR SETS & REPS

- 1st set   15 easy reps each arm
- 2nd set   12 moderate reps each arm
- 3rd set (optional)   10 hard reps each arm (work to failure)
- 4th set (optional)   8 to10 hard reps each arm (work to failure)

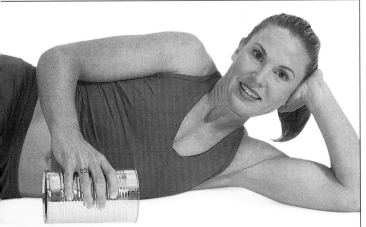

PROGRESSIONS

1 Start with a very light weight – golf ball, cricket ball, shoe, small can of food.

2 Increase weight slightly – large can of food, small water bottle etc.

3 Further increase weight – larger water bottle etc.

4 This exercise requires only a light weight. If you try to lift something too heavy you may compromise the value of the exercise and place these small stabilising muscles under too much stress.

BENCH OR CHAIR DIPS

Muscles involved: *triceps, pectorals, anterior deltoid.*

TARGET FOR SETS & REPS

- 1st set   15 easy reps
- 2nd set   12 moderate reps
- 3rd set (optional)   10 hard reps (work to failure)
- 4th set (optional)   8 to10 hard reps (work to failure)

PROGRESSIONS

1 Start with feet on the floor and legs bent at right angles.

2 Straighten legs and repeat movement.

3 Elevate feet on a seat, low table or a bench.

4 With your feet elevated, place a weight on your mid-section — sand bag, large water bottles etc.

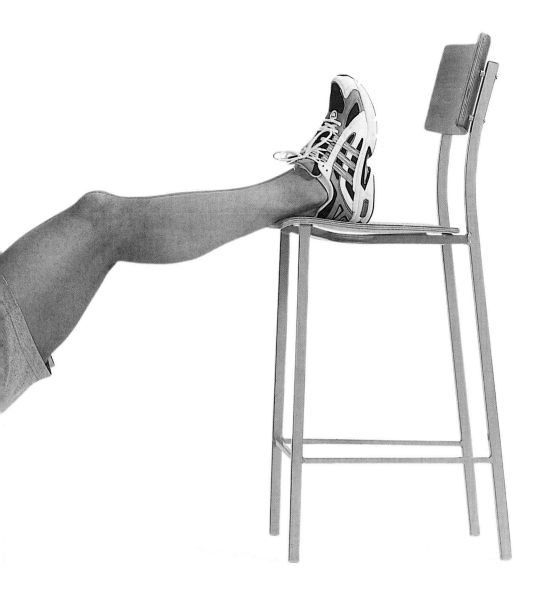

TECHNIQUE

1 Sit on a chair, bench or coffee table with your hands placed just wider than shoulder-width apart, face down and fingers forward over the edge of the bench.

2 Straighten your legs and slide your body forward so that your buttocks move just off the bench and your arms are supporting your weight.

3 From this starting position, slowly lower your body weight by bending your elbows.

4 Keep your head up, shoulders back, elbows back and fingers forward throughout the movement.

5 Lower yourself as far as possible, without taking your elbow joint past 90 degrees.

6 From the bottom of the movement push the heel of your hands down into the bench, straighten your elbows and return to the starting position.

7 Repeat the movement.

Bicep Curls

Muscles involved: *biceps and brachialis (forearm).*

Technique

1 Stand with a weight (such as a can of food) in either hand, arms by your side and legs slightly bent.

2 Activate your TVA and gluteals.

3 Grasp the weight with palms facing inward, toward your body.

4 Keeping your elbows in a relatively fixed position at the side of your body, bend your arms and raise the weight towards your shoulders until no further movement can occur.

5 As you raise the weights, rotate your forearms outwards so that your palms are now facing directly up.

6 Slowly lower your arms, rotating your forearm inwards, until you have returned to the starting position.

7 Repeat the movement.

8 The exercise can also be done by alternating your left and right arms. Otherwise the technique is the same.

Target for Sets & Reps

- 1st set   15 easy reps
- 2nd set   12 moderate reps
- 3rd set (optional)   10 hard reps (work to failure)
- 4th set (optional)   8 to10 hard reps (work to failure)

PROGRESSIONS

1 Progressions involve increasing the weights with each set.

2 Use aids such as cans of food, water bottles or full shopping bags.

SQUATS

Muscles involved: *gluteals,*
hamstrings, quadriceps, calves.

TECHNIQUE

1 Stand upright with your feet flat on the floor, slightly wider than shoulder-width apart and toes pointed out on a slight angle. Place your hands on your hips, by your side or crossed on your chest.

2 Keep your chin up and your eyes focussed straight ahead. Keep your shoulders back and chest out.

3 Activate your TVA.

4 Maintain a flat and relatively upright back throughout the movement.

5 From this starting position, bend your legs and lower your hips, in a controlled manner, towards the ground as if sitting in a low chair.

6 Aim for a position where your thighs are parallel to the ground.

7 From this position, push your heels directly into the ground and straighten your body back to the starting position.

8 It is vital that you keep your feet flat on the ground and your knees in direct line with your feet throughout the movement.

9 Repeat the movement.

TARGET FOR SETS & REPS

- 1st set   15 easy reps
- 2nd set   12 moderate reps
- 3rd set (optional)   10 hard reps (work to failure)
- 4th set (optional)   8 to10 hard reps (work to failure)

PROGRESSIONS

1 Add weight to increase the load.

2 Light weight can be held with arms by your side.

3 Moderate weight can held to your chest.

4 Heavier weight can be held above your head or on your shoulders.

LUNGE SQUATS

Muscles involved: *gluteals, hamstrings, quadriceps.*

TECHNIQUE

1 Stand in a wide lunge position with your right foot forward and left foot back. Make sure you have enough width between your legs for balance.

2 Lift your left foot up on to your toes and make sure it is pointing straight ahead.

3 Keep your head up and shoulders back. Make sure your hips are square on.

4 Activate and contract your left gluteal so that you feel a stretch through the hip flexor on the same leg.

5 From this starting position, slowly lower your left knee directly down to the floor.

6 Aim to stop your left knee just above the ground.

7 Your right knee should only move marginally and definitely not move past the toes on the right foot.

8 From this position, push your right heel into the ground, straighten your legs and return to the starting position.

9 Repeat the movement.

10 At the completion of the set with your right leg forward, repeat with your left.

TARGET FOR SETS & REPS

- 1st set   15 easy reps each leg
- 2nd set   12 moderate reps each leg
- 3rd set (optional)   10 hard reps each leg (work to failure)
- 4th set (optional)   8 to 10 hard reps each leg (work to failure)

PROGRESSIONS

1 Add weights to increase the load.

2 Light weight can be held with arms by your side.

3 Lunge squats have great potential for slow reps, partial reps and pause reps.

LOWER ABDOMINALS

There are many exercises for the abdominals. I have chosen one specifically aimed at strengthening the lower abdominal region and TVA, muscles largely responsible for lower back stabilisation. If you would like to add any others, feel free.

Muscles Involved: *transversus abdominis, rectus abdominis.*

TECHNIQUE

1 Lay on your back, on the floor, with legs bent and feet on the floor and close to your buttocks.

2 Activate your TVA.

3 Tilt your pelvis backwards and push your lower back hard into the floor.

4 Keeping legs bent and lower back pushing forcefully into the floor, slowly raise your left leg up and lower it down and then repeat with your right leg.

5 Repeat this movement.

6 Don't hold your breath.

7 Use a guide such as a rope, belt or your hands, placed under your back and directly below the navel to ensure that you are maintaining adequate pressure between your lower back and the floor.

8 You should be unable to pull this rope at any stage of the movement.

9 In this exercise, muscular failure occurs when you are no longer able to maintain adequate lower back pressure on the floor. To continue with exercise beyond this stage will cause potential harm to the lower back.

TARGET FOR SETS & REPS

- 1st set — 15 easy reps
- 2nd set — 12 moderate reps
- 3rd set (optional) — 10 hard reps (work to failure)
- 4th set (optional) — 8 to 10 hard reps (work to failure)

PROGRESSIONS

1 Start by adopting the position and holding for 30-60 seconds.

2 Alternately lift bent legs from the floor.

3 Start with knees back, legs at 90 degrees and feet off the floor. Slowly lower alternate bent legs to the floor and return.

4 Start as progression 3, but lower both feet to the floor together (keep legs bent).

5 As above, but gradually straighten legs.

6 It is crucial with this exercise that you do not progress until you have mastered the level you are on.

REVERSE HYPEREXTENSION

Muscles Involved*: gluteals, erector spinae (lower back)*

TECHNIQUE

1 Lay face-down on a table or desk so that you are securely holding on with your hands and your hips are just off the surface. You may need to place a pillow between your hips and the table for comfort.

2 Start with your legs straight and your toes on the floor.

3 By contracting your gluteals, raise your straight legs as high as possible.

4 Make sure your gluteals are as hard as possible.

5 Hold this position for two to three seconds and then slowly lower your toes back to the floor.

6 Repeat the movement.

TARGET FOR SETS & REPS

- 1st set   15 easy reps
- 2nd set   12 moderate reps
- 3rd set (optional)   10 hard reps (work to failure)
- 4th set (optional)   8 to10 hard reps (work to failure)

PROGRESSIONS

1 Start by lifting one leg at a time.

2 Lift both legs together.

3 Place a weight of some sort around your ankles or between your legs.

4 Increase the time of the hold at the top of the movement.

CIRCUITS

We all have different needs and lifestyles that dictate when and how we can include exercise. I know that, for most people, time is valuable and they don't want to waste it. So how can you structure the exercises included in this book so that they're not a huge time commitment, but you get maximum benefit from them?

BE ORGANISED

Get together all the props, equipment and weights you need for your session before you start so you are not wasting time during your workout. This will also ensure that the intensity of the session is not compromised.

THE FULL PROGRAM

If you go through the exercises in order, completing all sets of each exercise before moving on to the next, the program should take about 45-60 minutes. Stretching at the end will add another 10-15 minutes.

SUPER SETTING

This is a method of decreasing time and increasing the intensity of a workout. By choosing a pair of exercises and quickly alternating between the two you are able to save time that would normally be spent recovering between sets.

In the early stages you would choose two exercises that use different muscles. As you are performing one exercise the muscles used in the other are resting. As you progress and are looking for a harder workout, you may choose two exercises that use similar muscles.

The outline below is an example of how you might structure this super set session.

Pair one:	**Push Ups and Bent Over One Arm Row**
Pair two:	**Shoulder Press and Bicep Curls**
Pair three:	**Side Lying Rotator Cuff and Bench or Chair Dips**
Pair four:	**Squats and Reverse Hyperextensions**
Pair five:	**Lunge Squats and Lower Abdominals**

There are other ways to structure this session, this is just one example. This program should take about 30-40 minutes plus stretching.

If you've done one circuit and are feeling good, repeat the circuit or do a different one. Or you might try another circuit with a higher intensity of exercises.

Pair one: **Push Ups and Bent Over One Arm Row**

Pair two: **Shoulder Press and Bicep Curls**

SPLIT PROGRAM

This is a method to shorten the session time. It will however, double the number of workouts necessary. It involves splitting the program into two halves and completing each half alternately on different days. It's important that each half of the program involves different muscles, because training the same muscles on consecutive days will inhibit recovery and hence the overall result.

The following outline is an example of how you might structure this split workout:

Day one: **Push Ups, Bent Over One Arm Row and/or Body Weight Row, Shoulder Press, Bench or Chair Dips and Bicep Curls.**

Day two: **Side Lying Rotator Cuff, Squats, Lunge Squats, Lower Abdominals and Reverse Hyperextensions.**

Within this split workout it is also possible to super set. Each part of the workout should take about 25-35 minutes or 20-30 minutes if super setting, plus 10 minutes for stretching.

Whilst you are looking for a time-efficient workout, it is very important to accept that there is a minimum amount of time you must devote to your training if you are to get the most out of it.

There are 168 hours in a week and if you spend two or three hours on the *Simply Strength* program, you are devoting one to two per cent of your time to this life-changing plan. If you can't find that time, my guess is that you aren't really trying.

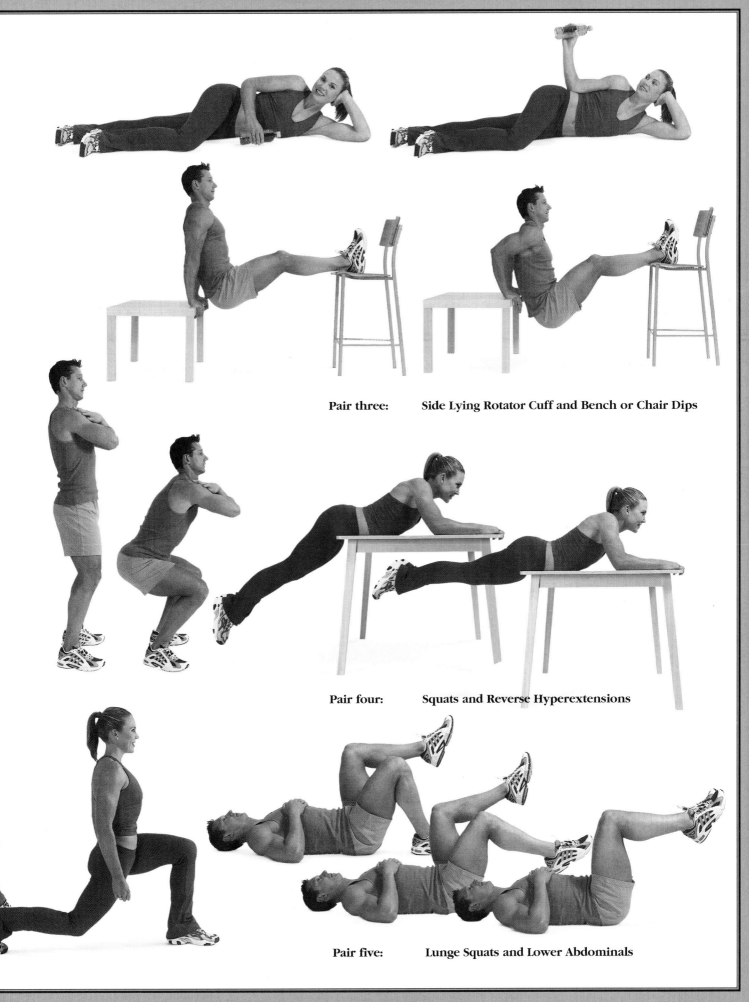

Pair three: Side Lying Rotator Cuff and Bench or Chair Dips

Pair four: Squats and Reverse Hyperextensions

Pair five: Lunge Squats and Lower Abdominals

STRETCHING OVERVIEW

Stretching is an important part of all exercise programs, yet it's neglected by most people. This can jeopardise the long-term effectiveness of your program. A commitment to spend 10-15 minutes stretching two or three times per week will create benefits that will make your exercise more effective, your body more supple and your life more enjoyable.

The best time to stretch your body is after training. This is because the muscles are already warm and more pliable and can therefore be moved further into positions where a long-term benefit can result.

The stretching program I am about to suggest includes six exercises. Only three of them should be done after every session, the remaining stretches need only be done after exercise using those specific muscles.

Each stretch needs to be performed correctly. For all strength exercises, technique is a priority to ensure full effect and to prevent injuries. Once you have achieved the correct stretch position, the following procedure must be followed for each stretch:

1 Take a deep breath in.

2 As you breathe out, move to the point of stretch.

3 Hold that position for 10-15 seconds.

4 Take in another deep breath.

5 As you breathe out, move even further into the stretch.

6 Hold for 10-15 seconds.

7 Repeat this once.

8 Come out of the stretch slowly using muscles other than those just stretched.

9 If you are tighter on one side than the other, do an extra 10-15 second hold on the tighter side.

THE STRETCHES

LOWER BACK ROTATION

Do this stretch after every session.

1 Lie on your back with your body straight and arms out at 90 degrees to your body.

2 Bend your left leg and keep your right leg straight.

3 Keep your shoulders flat on the floor and rotate your left leg across your body to the right.

4 Slide your right hip backwards so that your spine is in alignment.

5 You may use your right hand to push your left knee and increase the stretch.

6 Aim to get your left knee to the floor whilst keeping both shoulders flat on the floor.

7 Repeat on the other side.

HIP FLEXORS

Do this stretch after every session.

1 Kneel on both knees using a towel underneath for comfort.

2 Place your left foot forward, while remaining on your right knee.

3 Start with your right hip directly above your right heel.

4 Make sure your shoulders are back and your hips are square.

5 Contract your right gluteal and tuck your right hip under. This will initiate a stretch in the hip flexor.

6 Push forward through the hips, keeping your right gluteal 'tight and tucked', your body upright and your hips square.

7 Repeat with the right foot forward.

GLUTEALS

Do this stretch after every session.

1 Sit on the floor with both legs straight out in front of you.

2 Bend your left leg and put your left foot on the other side of your right leg.

3 Wrap your right arm around your left leg and pull it towards your chest.

4 Wrap your left arm tightly around your left leg and sit up bringing your shoulders back and square.

5 Repeat with the right leg.

STANDING QUADRICEPS

Do this stretch after leg strength and any cardio that involves legs.

1 Stand upright and lean against an immovable object.

2 Lift your left foot to your buttocks and grab it with your left hand.

3 Activate your left gluteal and pull your left foot straight back and up.

4 Keep your shoulders back and your knees close together throughout the stretch.

5 Repeat with the right leg.

CHEST AND BICEP

Do this stretch after upper body strength work or cardio involving the upper body

1 Stand about an arm's distance from an immovable object, such a doorway.

2 Place your left hand against the door edge, above shoulder height, with your thumb facing up.

3 Keeping your left arm straight, slowly rotate your body away from your left hand until you feel a stretch in the left chest region.

4 Repeat with the right arm.

TRICEPS AND UPPER BACK

Do this stretch after upper body strength work or cardio involving the upper body.

1 Stand up straight with both arms by your side.

2 Reach your left arm straight up and drop your left hand behind your head.

3 Grab your left elbow with your right hand and pull it across behind your head.

4 At the same time, bend your body sideways to the right.

5 Repeat with your right arm.

CARDIO TRAINING OVERVIEW

I have specifically spoken about strength training up to this point. As important as it is, it makes up only part of a well-balanced training routine.

For those of you who actually believe that the more sit-ups you do, the more fat you will burn off your stomach, or the more squats you do the leaner your buttocks will get, I have some bad news: it is not possible to spot reduce or to lose fat from a particular area simply by doing an exercise for that specific area. The strength exercise strengthens the muscle, which will contribute to an increased metabolism and hence overall long term fat burning. However, it won't cause fat to disappear from the particular area you are training.

The most effective way to become lean is by a combination of strength and cardiovascular training. The other vital ingredient to this process is adopting a sensible, enjoyable, healthy and energy-giving eating plan (see the 'Nutrition Overview' section later in this book).

Cardiovascular training, as the name suggests, involves the conditioning of the heart and lungs. It therefore has great benefits in heart health, oxygen uptake and utilisation, endurance, energy and fitness. The most favoured benefit of cardio training is the effect on metabolism and the body's use of fat as an energy source.

Q & A

Now for some answers to questions that are no doubt springing to your mind.

HOW OFTEN DO I NEED TO EXERCISE?

The answer to this question depends on what you are doing currently and what you have previously done. You will benefit from anything more than you are currently doing. So if you are doing no cardio training, then once or twice a week will be appropriate in the early stages (three to four cardio sessions per week would be ideal).

Remember that you have to be consistent, so whatever you decide in terms of frequency, you need to be able to maintain over the long term. Ensure that you consider your other commitments when making this decision.

Please do not fall in to the mentality of 'the more training the better'. If you over-train you will definitely not achieve your goals quicker. On the contrary, you might end up sore, tired, bored, frustrated, moody, injured, obsessive, carrying more fat and back to where you started.

HOW LONG SHOULD EACH EXERCISE SESSION BE?

The length of each session depends on your fitness level and the intensity of the session. Obviously, the more intense the session the shorter its duration can be. I would suggest that as a minimum for cardio training, 20-40 minutes would be appropriate. It's important that the intensity is appropriate for you to improve.

HOW HARD SHOULD I TRAIN?

If you want to improve, you need to exercise at a level that enables your muscles and energy systems to respond and adapt. If your exercise level is too easy, you won't get fitter, you will only maintain. If you push yourself too hard you are likely to end up injured, sick and back to where you started.

As a general rule, use the 'talk test'. If you can talk easily, your intensity is not high enough. If you can't talk at all, you are exercising too hard. If you can get words out in between some heavy breathing then your intensity is appropriate.

Start easy to moderate and gradually increase the intensity as you can. You increase cardiovascular intensity by going faster, going for longer or making the exercise more difficult. For example: let's say you can walk 5km in 45 minutes. To increase intensity, either walk 5km in 42 minutes, walk 6km or carry some hand weights for the 5km.

It really helps with your motivation and long-term results if you set yourself some short, medium and long-term goals.

If we use the example above: your short-term goal may be to walk 5 km in under 40 minutes (in one month). A medium-term goal may be to run 3 km without stopping (in three months). Your long-term goal may be to compete in a 6 km or 8 km fun run (in six months).

Once you can achieve these goals you will be amazed at how empowered you feel and how motivated you are to keep improving and achieving. Remember with all goals you set yourself, they need to be: realistic for you, challenging, specific and measurable, have a time frame and a set plan for their achievement.

WHERE DO I GO FROM HERE?

Make sure you choose activities that you enjoy, or at least enjoy the benefit of. Below is a list of cardiovascular exercises/sports. It is by no means exhaustive, you may have other suggestions or preferred activities. I have also included a recommended duration for a session of each particular exercise or activity.

Walking	**30-60 minutes**
Jogging/running	**15-40 minutes**
Cycling	**20-60 minutes**
Swimming	**20-40 minutes**
Skipping	**15-30 minutes**
Stair walking or running	**15-30 minutes**
Aerobics, spinning or water aerobics class	**45-60 minutes**
Tennis, squash, golf, touch rugby, bowls, cricket, football, netball, basketball, softball, baseball, soccer etc.	**30-60 minutes**
Boxing, martial arts, boxercise etc.	**30-60 minutes**

Again, it is vital for you to realise that you do not require a huge amount of time and money to get great results from cardio training. If you train at an appropriate level, then two to three sessions of 20-40 minutes duration are all that is required. Therefore, you are looking at a total of one to three hours of cardio training per week.

NUTRITION OVERVIEW

I've talked exclusively about exercise up to this point. It would, however, be irresponsible and remiss of me not to make mention of another highly crucial aspect. In fact, I will go so far as to say that I believe the quality of your nutrition determines the quality of your life.

When you stop and think about what you expect out of your body and what you put into it on a daily basis, you start to get an understanding about how you look and feel most of the time.

Ask yourself these questions:

- Do I regularly lack energy?
- Do I have trouble losing body fat or putting on muscle?
- Do I crave foods at particular times of the day?
- Do I have trouble concentrating?
- Am I moody or irritable more often than I would like to be?
- Do I lack motivation to exercise either first thing in the morning or at the end of a long day?
- Am I often too tired to enjoy my social life?
- Do I have difficulty sleeping?
- Do I have trouble dealing with stress?

If the answer to many of the above questions was yes, then ask yourself the following:

- Do I skip breakfast or eat it on the run?
- Do I work long hours?
- Do I go for more than three hours during the day without eating?

- Do I eat three meals or less per day?
- Do I binge eat in the afternoon and evening?
- Is dinner my largest meal of the day?
- Do I eat for convenience or for health?
- Do I eat a lot of processed foods?
- Is my eating sacrificed when my life is busy or stressful?

The first set of questions refer to symptoms that you may be experiencing. The second set of questions refer to actions or behaviours that may be contributing to the symptoms. All of which are related to the quality of your nutritional intake.

It is interesting to consider a little bit of history. In the 1970s there was a large shift in health focus towards an increase in exercise and a decrease in fat consumption. Whilst this focus has remained since that time, an even more interesting yet disturbing fact has become apparent. Australia today has the highest percentage of obesity ever recorded. In addition to this, the incidence of lifestyle diseases such as heart attacks and diabetes is more prevalent than ever.

In the same period of time we have also seen the development of technology and the 'it has to be done yesterday' attitude. This has created high-stress, limited time, fast food or even no-food lifestyle for many people.

We are generally aware of the amount of fat we are consuming. Unfortunately, we are not so familiar with the effects of an eating regime high in sugar, processed and artificial ingredients, as the abundance of quick, convenience and so-called health foods contain. My first piece of nutritional advice is: don't believe everything you see or hear. If something is advertised as low fat and healthy or endorsed by a celebrity, look at the ingredients and find out exactly what is in it to make it taste so similar to its higher fat equivalent.

Regardless of the amount of fat, sugar or whatever a product contains, if you do not eat enough food to cope with your daily energy requirements, you will face some serious health issues.

THE FACTS

The most basic reason for eating is to provide our body with the energy it needs to survive and excel day to day. The problem is that most people skip meals or make poor choices at the time of the day when they really need quality nutrition and energy. They then compound the problem by eating the majority of the food at the time of the day when they least need it.

The effect of not eating enough food when your energy requirements are high is significant. It creates the same situation that occurs when dieting by restricting calories, and can cause:

- a huge reduction in energy levels, performance and motivation
- an increase in moodiness and irritability
- a food deficient body will store fat and break down lean muscle for use as energy. This slows down metabolism, which in-turn will have serious long-term effects on the body's ability to burn fat
- a greater chance of binge eating at the end of the day
- a feeling of lack of control with food choices causing psychological, self-esteem and self-image issues.

The basic plan of your day must include:

1 Breakfast

2 Morning snacks (every 2-2.5 hours until lunch)

3 Lunch

4 Afternoon snacks (every 2-2.5 hours until dinner)

5 Small dinner.

The above plan ensures that you are eating food at the time of the day when your body needs energy. That is, as soon as you get up, during the morning and daytime. The evening meal, which is traditionally the largest, should be the smallest because it is the time of the day when you least need energy. A large meal at dinnertime followed by a long period of inactivity can only lead to the storage of body fat.

GENERAL NUTRITIONAL RULES

1 Follow the above plan, fitting the meals into your day as you can.

2 Be organised. Take food with you wherever you go so that you are never caught out without a healthy snack.

3 When shopping for food, carefully read labels and ingredient lists.

4 Eat mainly fresh and natural fruits and vegetables, quality proteins and whole grains instead of packaged and processed foods.

5 Try to reduce the amount of saturated and synthetic fats that you eat. Saturated fats are mostly found in animal and dairy products. Synthetic fats occur in many processed, takeaway and mass-produced foods.

6 Make sure you include some good fats in your eating regime as they are good for you in moderation. For example: fish (particularly salmon), olive, flaxseed or canola oil, avocado, almonds etc.

7 Do not reduce your carbohydrate intake, as this is your body's preferred energy source. Instead, try to eat natural, fresh, whole-grain carbohydrates, reduce the amount of highly refined, processed and sugar-filled carbohydrates, even if they are low in fat, and eat the majority of your carbohydrates in the morning and during the day.

8 Eat only a small amount of carbohydrates in the evening.

9 Eat lots of green vegetables and salads.

10 Try to include some protein with most meals.

11 If you are vegetarian make sure you are getting enough protein and iron.

12 Drink lots of water, ideally two to three litres per day.

13 Decrease the amount of caffeine you drink. Aim for no more than two cups of coffee or tea per day.

14 Enjoy your indulgences in moderation.

MEAL SUGGESTIONS

BREAKFAST IDEAS

- Whole grain cereals (muesli, oats and other similar types) with low fat milk, fresh fruit and/or low fat yoghurt.
- Toast (soy & linseed, rye, sourdough rye, multi grain) with any combination of: low fat cottage cheese, poached or boiled eggs (one yolk only), lean ham, avocado (instead of butter/margarine), tomato, tuna, vegemite, jam (no added sugar), peanut butter (in moderation) etc.

MORNING SNACK IDEAS

- Fresh fruit.
- Low fat yoghurt.
- Almonds, seeds and dried fruit mix.
- Natural whole grain cracker biscuits (with toppings as above).
- Smoothie – with low fat milk, yoghurt, fruit and possibly protein powder.

LUNCH IDEAS

- Sandwiches, rolls and/wraps with lean meat, chicken, turkey, tuna, cheese, eggs with avocado and salad.
- Salads with chicken, lamb, tuna etc. Be sure to include some carbohydrate with this meal. For example: sweet potato, rice, bread.
- Whole grain pasta with a tomato-based sauce.
- Soups with whole grain bread.
- Whole grain rice dishes with protein and vegetables.

AFTERNOON SNACK IDEAS

• As for morning snack.

DINNER IDEAS

• Barbecued or grilled chicken, fish, steak with salads
  or vegetables.

• Stir fries with protein and vegetables.

• Casseroles.

• Soups.

• Omelettes.

• Reduce the amount of starches (pasta, rice, potatoes,
  bread etc) at this time with a view to eliminating them.

AFTER DINNER

• Avoid eating after dinner.

• If you are generally hungry after dinner, eat more
  during the day.

• Enjoy an occasional snack or dessert.

VEGETARIAN PROTEINS

• Tofu, soy beans, tempeh, miso, chick peas, lentils,
  beans and nuts.

• To ensure effective absorption of these plant proteins,
  combine them with whole grains such as rice, pasta
  and bread.

SUGGESTED SPREADS SAUCES & FLAVOURS

• Vegemite, jams (no added sugar), almond/peanut
  spread (in moderation), avocado etc.

• Soy sauce/Tamari (no added sugar), lemon juice,
  mustard, chutney (no added sugar), red wine, curry
  powder, tomato paste, herbs and spices.

RECORD-KEEPING

Your decision to buy this book and change your life is a fantastically empowering one. I hope that the program and suggestions seem manageable to you.

Remember the goal is long-term results.

As motivated as you may feel right at this moment, don't expect to feel that way every day. When the novelty wears off and the weather turns sour, that is the time you need to stick firmly to your goals and believe in yourself.

It's all about small steps toward a final aspiration. You will make mistakes along the way – you are human. One way of ensuring that you do keep improving is by keeping an accurate record of your exercise and your eating.

You can continually set yourself goals if you know what you have previously done.

The following are sample record-keeping pages for your exercise and your food, which I invite you to copy for your own use.

STRENGTH RECORD

DAY . . . . DATE . . / . . / . .

EXERCISE	WEIGHTS & REPS									
	1	2	3	4	5	6	7	8	9	10

CARDIO RECORD

DAY . . . . DATE . . ./. . ./. . .

EXERCISE	AMOUNT (TIME, DISTANCE, RESISTANCE ETC.)

FOOD RECORD

DAY . . . . DATE . . /. . /. . .

TIME	QTY	DESCRIPTION

Water Consumed (glasses)	1	2	3	4	5	6	7	8	9	10
Mood:	Excellent		Good		Fair		Poor			
Energy Levels:	Very High		High		Moderate	Low				

GLOSSARY

Consistency   following a plan regularly

Load   the resistance applied to each exercise

Long-term   making changes and creating habits that can be maintained forever

Progressions   slightly varying the exercise to increase the load

Progressive overload   gradual increase of intensity for an exercise over time

Repetitions (reps)   each complete repeat of a movement

Sets   each group of repetitions

Super sets   pairing exercises and alternating sets between them to save time

CONCLUSION

The endeavour to improve health, get lean, be fitter, increase strength and look a certain way has been a long-term pursuit for millions of people over many years. For the majority, these attempts have been futile for one simple reason: an inability to maintain the exercise and/or eating regime over an extended period.

The first step to long-term success is to understand what is required. The second vital ingredient is to develop a plan that you can maintain consistently. The third step is to make the plan a priority in your life and take the time and effort to establish it as your normal weekly routine.

Simply Strength has provided you with the knowledge, the exercises and strategies for long-term achievement. The rest is up to you.

Have faith in yourself, you have the ability to be or do anything you desire (within reason).

I'm sure that this attempt to look, feel and perform at your very best will be successful.

About the Authors

SALLY JOBLING has established herself as a health professional providing valuable education to athletes, sporting groups and individuals, assisting and supporting them to reach their full potential.

Sally has had personal success in a number of sporting fields from an early age. She competed at state level for athletics, has placed in the top 5% in a number of fun runs, was in the top three for her age group for triathlon and recently completed her first marathon along with a number of clients she prepared for the event.

Sally's passion for creating healthy meals lead her to co-found Twist Pty Ltd. Sally has been instrumental in the design of many of the Twist recipes and is currently compiling a book of favourites. Through Twist, Sally continues to work closely with athletes and individuals designing eating plans.

ANDREW JOBLING completed a Bachelor of Education (Physical Education) at Victoria College in Melbourne. Since that time he has accumulated over 20 years of experience in the education, health, strength and fitness industry. In that time he has taught Physical Education to secondary students, worked in public gyms as an instructor and he has operated as a personal trainer for over 12 years. Since 1999 he has been a director of Harper's Personal Training, one of the largest personal training businesses in Australia. In 2000 he was founder/director of Twist Pty Ltd, a company dedicated to educating people about the enormous power of food and providing them with delicious and healthy meals.

Andrew has worked with many people in fitness and strength. His involvement with the St Kilda Australian Rules Football Club began as a player in the 1980s, and since then he has helped many high-level athletes with their strength and conditioning. The list includes athletes from several AFL clubs, Port Melbourne Football Club (VFL), Melbourne Phoenix Netball Club (Australian National League premiers), and professional golfers, just to name a few. He has designed and implemented programs for thousands of people to help them achieve their health and fitness goals, not just for a month or a year but for their whole lives.